Our Planet Earth

Claire Llewellyn

Scholastic
Reference

SCHOLASTIC INC.

New York Toronto London Auckland Sydney

How to use this book

Look it up!

Our Planet Earth tells you all about Earth, its surface, the way it changes, and many of the plants and animals that live here. The Contents page at the front of the book lists all of the subjects, or entries, discussed in the book and on which pages they begin.

Cross-references

Above the colored bar on each page there is a list of related entries in this book or any of the other four books in the *Scholastic First Encyclopedia* series, with their book titles. These other entries tell you more about the subject on the page. If there are a lot of related entries, only the book title is given. Entries in *A First Atlas* are listed by the map headings. You will be able to find out more information in the section that follows the given map heading.

Glossary

Words in the book that may be difficult to understand are written in **bold**. The Glossary, which starts on page 72, lists these words in alphabetical order and explains what they mean.

Index

The Index, which starts on page 74, is a list of many of the things mentioned in the book, arranged in alphabetical order, with their page numbers. If you want to read about a subject, look it up in the Index and then turn to the page number given. When a page number is written in *italics*, there will be a picture of the entry on that page.

Contents

How Earth began

Earth is a huge rocky ball traveling through space. Its story started a very long time ago when the universe began. Scientists think that about 15 **billion** years ago there was a huge explosion, called the Big Bang. Slowly, over many billions of years, stars and **planets** began to form. One of the stars was the Sun, and one of the planets was Earth.

▶ Earth is one of a group of nine planets in space that travel around the Sun.

The story of Earth

❶ Earth formed about 4.5 billion years ago. Pieces of dust were pulled together, making a hot, rocky ball.

❷ As Earth slowly cooled, a thin, hard crust formed on its surface.

❸ After millions of years, clouds formed in the air and the first rain fell.

❹ Rainwater filled the deepest hollows on Earth's surface. This made the ocean.

Earth's structure

Earth is made up of different layers of rock and metal. The crust is the hard, rocky layer on which people live. Below this is the mantle, which is a thick layer of rock. It is so hot that some of it has melted, making it move slowly. In the middle of Earth lies the metal core. The core has two layers. The outer core is **liquid**, but the inner core is **solid** and hard.

crust

mantle

outer core

inner core

▶ As you travel through the different layers, Earth becomes hotter and hotter.

Life on Earth

Animals and plants live almost everywhere on Earth's surface. This is because Earth is just the right distance from the Sun, and is neither too hot nor too cold. The first living things appeared over 3 billion years ago. They were **bacteria** that lived in Earth's ocean.

Did you know?

Earth's center is about 100 times hotter than the hottest desert!

In most places, Earth's crust is only about 22 miles deep. Compared to the whole planet, it is very thin — sort of like the skin on a peach.

Long ago, people believed Earth was flat. They thought that if ships sailed too far, they would fall off the edge.

See also Earthquake, Fossil, Ocean exploration, Rock, Wind

Studying Earth

Scientists study Earth by exploring its different layers. They investigate the surface and deep underground. There is still so much to learn about Earth that many scientists study one particular subject, such as earthquakes, rocks, or weather.

▼ Water from the Arctic Ocean is collected in bottles by a diver. Then it is taken away to be tested.

Looking at rocks and fossils
Scientists who study rocks are called geologists. They work like detectives, examining rocks for clues, such as fossils, which are the remains of dead plants and animals. These help geologists learn more about Earth.

The moving Earth
Seismologists are scientists who study sudden movements in Earth's crust called earthquakes. They use an instrument called a seismograph to measure how strong an earthquake is and to find out where it is happening.

Watching the weather

Meteorologists are scientists who study the weather. They learn about the weather with the help of aircraft and balloons. These carry special instruments that send information back to weather stations on the ground.

Meteorologists can make weather **forecasts** by gathering information about air **pressure**, wind, clouds, and air **temperature** from all over the world.

▲ Meteorologists sometimes release weather balloons into storms. The instruments on board measure how hot or cold the air is and the strength of the wind.

Satellites

Satellites are machines that are sent into space. They circle Earth and look down on the **planet**. Weather satellites take pictures of cloud patterns. Other satellites look at Earth's surface. They may measure the size of a rainforest or show how well crops are growing.

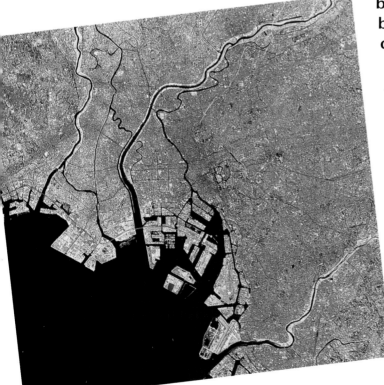

◀ A satellite took this photograph of Tokyo, the capital city of Japan. The city's three main rivers can be seen flowing to the sea.

Ocean exploration

People have traveled the ocean for thousands of years. About 500 years ago, they began to explore under the water, using simple **craft** called diving bells. These held enough air for a person to breathe underwater for just a few minutes. In the last 50 years, modern breathing equipment and diving craft have made it possible for people to stay underwater for much longer.

Studying the ocean

Scientists who study the ocean are called oceanographers. They work on ships and carry out experiments on rocks, water, and mud which they collect from the ocean. They also measure the depth of the water and draw maps of the ocean floor.

▶ Divers use waterproof cameras and lights to take photographs of parts of the ocean and the creatures that live here.

Using sonar

Scientists can find out the depth of the ocean by using sonar. On a ship, sonar equipment sends down a burst of sound to the ocean floor.

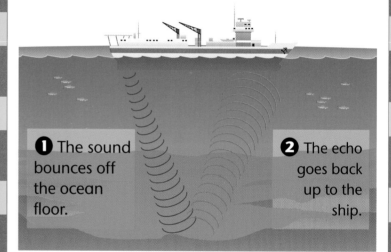

❶ The sound bounces off the ocean floor.

❷ The echo goes back up to the ship.

By counting the time it takes for the sound to travel down and for the echo to bounce back, scientists can tell how far down the floor lies.

Exploring the deep

Scientists explore the ocean floor in diving craft called submersibles. Some of these submersibles can dive up to 13,000 feet deep. Submersibles have to be strong or they will be crushed by the powerful **pressure** of the water. Some of these craft carry people, but most are controlled by scientists from ships on the surface of the ocean.

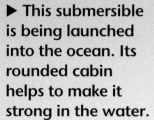 **now picture this** In the deepest parts of the ocean, water pressure is so great that it is like being squeezed by ten elephants.

▲ *Alvin* is a submersible that has made hundreds of dives to the ocean floor. It is fitted with powerful lights and a metal arm for collecting samples.

▶ This submersible is being launched into the ocean. Its rounded cabin helps to make it strong in the water.

Continent

A continent is a huge area of land. Most of the land that makes up a continent is in one large piece, but nearby islands are also often part of a continent. For example, the United Kingdom is part of the continent of Europe. Earth has seven continents. They cover just over one quarter of Earth's surface. The rest is covered by water. Together, the continents could all easily fit into the Pacific, the world's largest ocean.

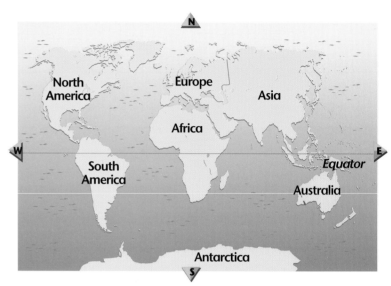

▲ The largest continent in the world is Asia. The smallest continent is Australia.

Drifting continents

Earth's continents and the ocean floor are made of huge pieces of rock called **plates**. These plates float gently on Earth's slow-moving mantle below.

▼ On this map, the continent of Africa and its plate have been lifted off the mantle to show that Africa is huge but its plate is even bigger.

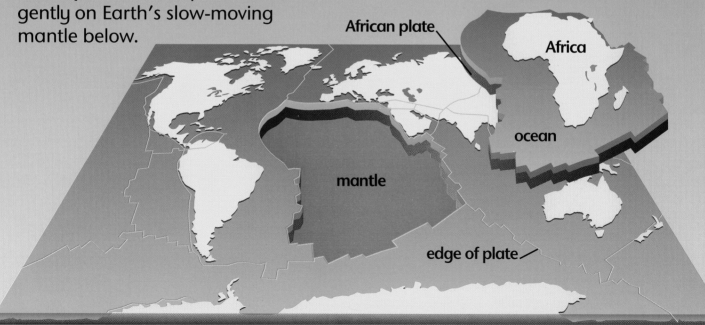

◀ In Iceland, a deep rift has formed where two of Earth's plates have slowly drifted apart.

▼ The Himalayas were formed when two plates bumped together and forced the rock into huge mountains.

Plate problems

Earth's plates are moving slowly and can bump into one another. This causes movements inside Earth which are sometimes powerful enough to create an earthquake, a volcano, or a mountain. Earth's plates can also pull apart from each other, making a deep cut in the land called a rift.

How Earth has changed

Scientists believe that about 200 million years ago, all of Earth's land was joined together in one big piece. Slowly, the land broke up into continents.

This is how the continents look today. You can see how the coasts of Africa and South America could have once fitted together like pieces of a puzzle.

Africa

South America

Ocean

The ocean is one huge body of saltwater that surrounds Earth's continents. The ocean has four main regions: Pacific, Atlantic, Indian, and Arctic. The ocean covers so much of the **planet** that Earth looks blue from space. Thousands of plants and animals live in the ocean. They come in a wide range of colors and sizes.

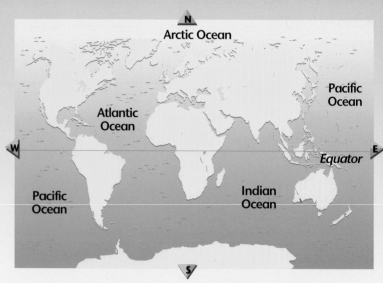

▲ The biggest ocean is the Pacific. It is larger than all the others put together.

The ocean floor

On the ocean floor, there are mountains, hills, and **valleys**, just as there are on land.

Near the shore, the land slopes gently into the water. This area is called the continental shelf. It then falls steeply away.

Thousands of volcanoes, called sea mounts, lie under the ocean.

Long, narrow trenches cut down through the ocean floor. Some of them are nearly 7 miles deep. They are the deepest parts of the ocean.

A huge flat plain covers about half the ocean floor. On top of it lies a thick layer of mud, sand, and the remains of tiny plants and sea animals.

Text: Claire Llewellyn
Consultants: Graham Peacock and Terry Hudson
Computer illustrations: Mel Pickering
Watercolor illustrations: Colin King
Photo research: Lyndsey Price

Art Director: Belinda Webster
Production Director: Lorraine Estelle
Managing Editor: Deborah Kespert
Editor: Samantha Hilton
Designer: Lisa Nutt

U.S. Editorial Team
Executive Editor: Carolyn Jackson
Science consultant: Gary Brockman

Photo credits: Brian & Cherry Alexander: p52; Allsport: p50 (bottom); BBC Natural History Unit/Martha Holmes: p36; Britstock IFA: p49 (bottom); Bruce Coleman: p18, p19, p25 (top), p37 (bottom), p48 (top), p51, p53 (top), p58, p59, p61 (top), p62 (bottom right), p64, p66, p67 (bottom), p68; Robert Harding: p15 (top left), p21, p22/23 (center), p26, p42, p44 (top); Hutchinson Library/Robert Francis: p41 (bottom right); Images Colour Library: p28/29 (center); Images of Africa Photobank/David Keith Jones: p35; NHPA: p12, p22 (bottom left), p33, p45 (right); Oxford Scientific Films: p13 (top and bottom), p15 (top right), p24, p27 (top and bottom), p29 (right), p54 (bottom), p56 (bottom), p63, p67 (top), p69 (right); Pictor: p49 (top); Planet Earth: p17, p31 (right), p32, p48 (bottom), p60/61 (center), p62 (bottom left), p65; Science Photo Library: p11 (top and bottom), p55, p57; SPL/Jim Amos: p25 (bottom); SPL/Eye of Science: p43; SPL/Peter Menzel: p39; Still Pictures/Mark Edward: p71; Telegraph Colour Library: p56 (top), p69 (left), p70 (bottom center); Tony Stone: p10, p31 (center), p38, p44/45 (center), p53 (bottom), p70/71 (center); Zefa: p8, p20, p23 (bottom right), p28 (left), p30/31 (center), p34 (left and right), p37 (top), p40, p41, p46, p47, p50 (top), p54 (top), p61 (bottom right).

Produced for Scholastic Inc. by Two-Can Publishing Ltd., 346 Old Street, London, EC1V 9NQ, U.K.
Copyright © 1997 by Scholastic Inc. and Two-Can Publishing Ltd.
All rights reserved. Published by Scholastic Inc.

No part of this publication may be reproduced, or stored in a retrieval system, or transmitted in any form or by any means, electronic, mechanical, photocopying, recording, or otherwise, without written permission of the publisher. For information regarding permission, write to Scholastic Inc., 555 Broadway, New York, NY 10012.

Library of Congress Cataloging-in-Publication Data

    Llewellyn, Claire
    Our planet earth / [Claire Llewellyn]
        p.   cm. — (Scholastic first encyclopedia)
    Includes index
    Summary: Looks at earth, how it was formed, the way it changes,
    and some of the plants and animals that live there.
    ISBN 0-590-87929-4
    1. Earth sciences—Juvenile literature.   2. Earth—Juvenile literature.
    [1. Earth sciences. 2. Earth.] I. Title. II. Series.
    QE29. L62 1997
    550—dc21   97-12561
                                CIP
                                AC

12 11 10 9 8 7 6 5 4 3 2   8 9 0/0 01 02

Color reproduction by Daylight Colour Art Pte Ltd., Singapore.
First Scholastic printing, September 1997.

Moving water

Ocean water is constantly moving. Great bands of water, called currents, flow like rivers through the ocean. Warm currents flow away from the **Equator**, and cool ones flow away from the North and South **Poles**.

On the surface of the ocean, the wind blows the water into waves. Near the shore, the waves pound the land. Waves churn up the water, spreading food and **oxygen** for animals and plants to the deepest parts of the ocean.

▲ The ocean is home to over 13,000 different types of fish. These fish, called groupers, live in warm waters.

Some sea mounts are so high that they stick out of the water.

A long line of underwater mountains runs along the middle of the ocean. This is called the midocean ridge.

Did you know?

The Mariana Trench in the Pacific Ocean is 7 miles deep. You could fit Mount Everest inside it and still have room to spare.

Surfers flock to Hawaii, where the waves can be 30 feet high. That's more than five times the height of a man.

The Arctic Ocean is usually covered by a layer of ice over 12 feet thick.

Island

An island is a piece of land entirely surrounded by water. It can be as small as a house or it can be a huge area of land with towns, mountains, and forests. Most islands are small and are scattered in groups through the ocean. Some are thousands of miles from the **mainland** and people do not live here.

Undersea volcanoes

Some islands are formed by volcanoes under the ocean. When an underwater volcano **erupts**, it throws up a mixture of hot rock and ash. This hardens where it falls which makes the volcano grow higher. Eventually, after thousands of years, it breaks through the surface of the water and forms an island.

▲ Mooréa is an island in the Pacific Ocean formed by a volcano. Most people live on the flat land near the coast.

A coral atoll

An atoll is an island in the shape of a ring. It is made mostly from coral, which is a **material** formed from tiny living and dead sea creatures. Atolls are found in **tropical** waters. Below you can see how an atoll forms.

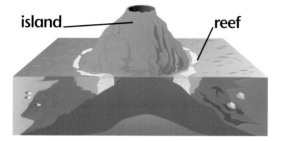

island————————reef

Coral begins to grow around the edges of a tropical island, forming a **coral reef**.

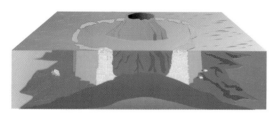

The island slowly begins to sink beneath the water. The coral piles up and the reef grows bigger.

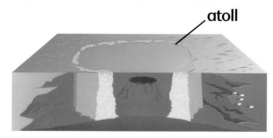

atoll

Eventually, the island disappears completely beneath the waves. All that is left is a ring of coral, or atoll.

Breaking away

Some islands were once part of large continents. When the ocean waters rose, they **flooded** the lower parts of the land. Today, only the high parts of the land can be seen above the water. Other islands became separated from large continents when movements in Earth's **plates** caused the land to break off and drift away.

Life on an island

Animals and plants that live on an island are often different from those found in other places. Over millions of years, they have slowly changed to suit the **environment** in which they live.

▲ Tortoises from the Galápagos Islands are much bigger than tortoises from other parts of the world. They can weigh as much as seven children.

Mountain

A mountain is a high hill with a steep slope. Most mountains are found in long lines, called ranges, which were formed many millions of years ago. Mountains are always slowly changing. They can become taller or be worn down by ice, snow, and mountain streams.

▶ Mountain ranges are found on every continent in the world. The largest range is in Asia. It is 1,500 miles long.

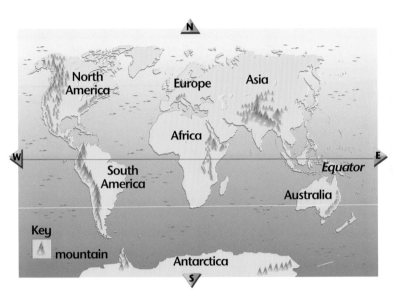

Making mountains

Mountain ranges are made by Earth's **plates**. Where two plates meet, they sometimes push hard against each other.

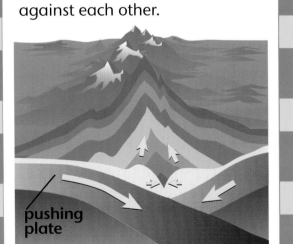

pushing plate

Slowly, over millions of years, the land buckles up into huge folds of rock, which we call mountains.

Mountains and people

Life can be hard in the mountains, so few people live here. Most villages spring up between mountains. The high peaks form a barrier between the villages. Bridges and tunnels make mountains easier to cross, but in some places the only way to travel is on foot.

▲ The mountain people of Tibet are skilled in living high up. They raise herds of yaks for their milk and meat.

▼ It is so cold on the tops of some mountains that they are covered with snow even in the summer.

Animals and plants

As you climb up a mountain, the air becomes colder and the kinds of plants begin to change. On the lower slopes, forests are home to many animals. Higher up, the air becomes too cold for trees, and only a few mosses and grasses are able to survive. Animals, such as mountain goats, wildcats, and eagles, live high on the mountains.

See also Continent, Desert, Erosion, Mountain; ANIMALS AND NATURE Earth; HOW THINGS WORK Metal

Rock

Rock is the hard, **solid** part of the land and makes up Earth's crust. In some places on Earth, the rock is covered by a layer of soil in which trees and other plants can grow. In other parts, it is covered by the ocean. But in a few places, such as deserts and mountains, the rock is bare.

▶ Boulders, such as the Devil's Marbles in Australia, are rocks that have been worn smooth and round by wind and rain.

All kinds of rocks

Different kinds of rocks are made up of different mixtures of **minerals**. Some minerals are soft and crumbly. Others are hard and shiny. Some minerals form gemstones, such as diamonds, inside rock.

▲ Opal is a gemstone.
It can be cut out of rock and then polished.

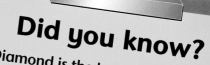

Did you know?

Diamond is the hardest **material** in the world. It is used on drill tips to cut through rock. Diamond can also be made into scalpels and used by surgeons during hospital operations.

Talcum powder is made from talc, the world's softest mineral.

You eat at least one kind of mineral every day — salt.

Using rocks

Rocks are useful materials.

Granite is a hard rock that is often used to make buildings.

Teachers use sticks of chalk to write on a blackboard.

Gemstones are made into all sorts of jewelry.

Ores
Some rocks contain metals, such as iron. These rocks are called ores. Iron ore is dug up from mines and crushed. The iron is removed and made into tools or steel.

Rocks for building
Rocks used for building are taken from large pits called quarries, which are often dug into the sides of mountains. Huge pieces of rock are cut out of the quarries and made into smaller slabs.

▲ At a quarry, powerful machines are used to lift slabs of rock onto trucks, which will carry them to building sites.

See also Ocean, Rock; ANIMALS AND NATURE Earth

Fossil

When an animal or plant dies, it sometimes leaves a mark or its remains in a rock. This is called a fossil. Many fossils are of animals that lived in the ocean. Other fossils include plants and the footprints or bones of animals, such as dinosaurs. Many fossils are millions of years old.

How a fossil forms

When a dead animal sinks to the bottom of an ocean, river, or swamp, it becomes covered by layers of mud and sand. The animal's soft parts rot away, leaving only its bones behind.

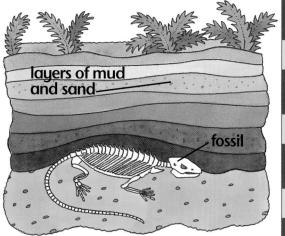

layers of mud and sand

fossil

Over millions of years, the many layers of mud and sand harden into rock and the bones turn to stone. This is one way a fossil forms.

▶ Ancient plants, such as tree ferns, leave their stem and vein marks in rock to make a fossil.

The oldest fossils

Scientists study fossils to help them learn about the kinds of creatures that lived in the past. Many of these creatures are **extinct** today. The oldest fossils of hard-shelled animals were formed about 600 million years ago.

A fossil timeline

1 600 million years ago, creatures called trilobites made their homes in the ocean.

2 400 million years ago, the first fish appeared on Earth.

Life in the past

Many living things do not turn into fossils. Some creatures, such as worms, have completely soft bodies, so all their parts rot away before a fossil can form. This makes it hard for scientists to find out about all the animals that lived on Earth in the past. There are gaps in the story.

▶ Ammonites were ancient creatures that lived inside shells in the ocean.

❸ 310 million years ago, huge dragonflies flew over Earth's swamps.

❹ 180 million years ago, an animal called an ichthyosaur lived in the ocean.

❺ 150 million years ago, a plant-eating dinosaur named brachiosaurus lived on the land.

Fossil hunting

Scientists search for fossils in ancient rocks. When they find a fossil, they dig it out slowly and carefully. Then they cover it with plaster to protect it and take it to a museum. Here, scientists clean and study the fossil.

▶ This scientist is gently chipping away at a large, fossilized dinosaur bone. Other bones are still buried in the rock.

River

now picture this

The world's shortest river is the D River in Oregon. It is only about 40 yards long — the length of 25 salmon swimming nose to tail.

A river is a large stream of water that flows into a **lake** or an ocean. As a river moves along, it changes the shape of the land by picking up mud and stones and dropping them in different places. A river is important because it gives people clean water and food. Many animals and plants make their homes in a river.

A river's journey

A river usually begins its journey high in the hills, where rain trickles into streams. The streams flow into one another, making a fast-flowing river that races down the hillside. On flatter land, the river moves more slowly. It becomes bigger and wider as it winds its way to an ocean or lake.

▼ Smaller rivers, called tributaries, carry water to larger rivers.

Using rivers

For thousands of years people have made good use of rivers.

People eat fish, such as trout, salmon, and eels, from rivers.

Boats and barges carry goods from place to place.

In dry places, water is made to flow along channels so farmers can water their crops. This is called irrigation.

▲ When a river runs over a steep cliff, it forms a waterfall. Most waterfalls are found high in the mountains, near the start of a river's journey.

River life

All kinds of animals live in and around rivers, including worms, snails, insects, fish, snakes, and frogs. Some fish, such as trout, live in fast-flowing streams. Other fish, such as perch, prefer slow-moving rivers. Plants, such as water lilies and duckweeds, grow in rivers. They provide food for animals that live in the river and along its banks.

▲ Otters are at home in rivers. They live in dens along riverbanks and feed mainly on fish.

Forest

A forest is a large area of land where trees grow closely together. Different kinds of forest, including rainforest, are found all over the world. They make a good home for many animals and plants.

Two kinds of forest

In cool parts of the world, there are two kinds of forest, deciduous and coniferous. Trees in a deciduous forest have wide, flat leaves, which fall off the branches in autumn. Coniferous trees have thin leaves called needles. Most coniferous trees keep their leaves all year.

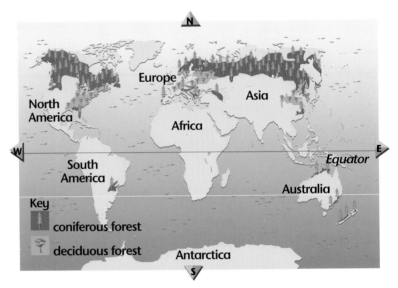

▲ Most coniferous forests grow in the northern part of the world. Deciduous forests grow farther south.

▼ The leaves of deciduous trees turn yellow, red, and gold before they die and fall to the ground.

▲ Winters are harsh in a coniferous forest. The trees' smooth needles and sloping branches help them shed the heaviest snow.

Using the forests

Forests provide people with foods and all sorts of other useful things.

Wood is used to make many things, such as furniture, pencils, and toys.

Paper is made from wood that is mashed into pulp, pressed flat, and dried.

The corks we push into bottles are made from the soft bark of the cork oak tree.

The fruits and nuts of a forest make healthy, delicious foods.

▲ Chipmunks live in the forests of North America. They feed on seeds and nuts.

The forest web

All the animals and plants in a forest need each other. The leaves, fruits, and seeds of forest plants provide food for plant-eating animals, such as worms and mice. In turn, they are eaten by meat-eaters such as foxes and owls.

See also Climate and season, Forest, Human; ANIMALS AND NATURE Forest; A FIRST ATLAS Tropical South America

Tropical rainforest

Tropical rainforests are thick, damp forests with tall trees and big, colorful flowers. Tropical rainforests grow near the Equator, where it is hot and wet all year round. They have given people many useful things, such as rubber, chocolate, and medicines.

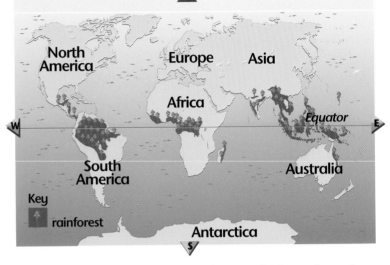

Key
rainforest

▲ The largest rainforest is in South America along the Amazon River. It crosses several countries.

Forest layers

A rainforest is like a three-story building. Each story has its own animals and plants.

The canopy is the top story. The tallest tree tops are here.

The understory has smaller trees and bushes.

The dark forest floor is home to mosses and **fungi**.

▶ Many rivers run through a rainforest. They are often the only way to travel from one part to another.

Life in the rainforests

Rainforests are full of animal life, including many types of insects. High in the canopy, monkeys shriek and birds call. Lower down, frogs and snakes live in the trees, while big cats, such as jaguars, hunt on the ground.

Different groups of people live in the rainforests. Some survive by hunting animals and gathering plants to eat. Others grow crops.

▶ A sloth spends most of its life feeding on leaves of rainforest trees.

▲ The Machiguenga Indians live in the Amazon rainforest. They eat fruit, such as papaya, collected from trees.

The future of the forests

In the last 50 years, people have been chopping down rainforests to make room for farmland and mines. Plants and animals have lost their homes and some have become **extinct**. Today, people understand the damage this has done and are protecting the forests that remain.

Plain

A plain is a large area of mainly flat land covered by grasses. Only a few scattered trees and small bushes grow here. Most plains are dry places, where rain falls for only part of the year.

Animals on the plains
The plains provide food for many different plant-eating animals, such as zebras and wildebeest. In turn, they are hunted by meat-eating animals, such as hyenas, lions, and cheetahs.

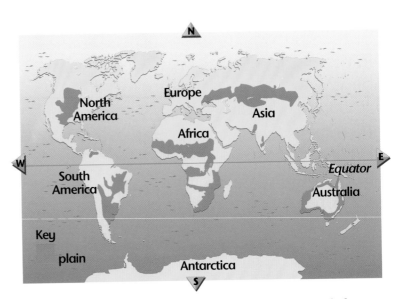

▲ The plains have different names around the world. In Africa they are called savannah, while in Asia their name is steppe. Prairies stretch across North America, and pampas cover South America.

▼ There are few places to hide on the African savannah. Zebras live in large groups, called herds, to protect themselves from hunting animals, such as lions.

32

How grass grows

Grasses are tough plants. They can survive fires on the plains and heavy **grazing** by animals. Many grasses have lots of roots that lie protected deep under the ground, so new shoots can grow from the bottom of the plants if the old shoots die. When it rains, grasses grow green and tall, but if the weather becomes too dry, they may wither.

▶ A weaver bird loops and knots grass to build its nest.

now picture this

Pampas grass grows up to 9 feet high — as tall as two children, one on top of the other.

Using the plains

Grassland soil is so **fertile** that many plains have been taken over by farmers for growing food or grazing farm animals.

Farmers grow wheat and corn on large parts of the North American prairies.

There are huge sheep farms on the Australian grasslands.

Much of the pampas in South America is used for raising cattle.

Nomads in Africa graze their animals on the dry savannah.

33

Desert

A desert is a dry place where it hardly ever rains. Only a few living things can survive here. Desert plants and animals are **adapted** to life in the dry climate. Some plants, such as cacti, store large amounts of water. Many animals, such as gerbils, come out to feed only during the cool of the night.

A desert climate

In many deserts, the days are burning hot. But after sunset, the **temperature** can drop quickly, so the nights can be frosty and cold. The little rain that does fall in deserts soon dries up on the land, or soaks deep into the ground.

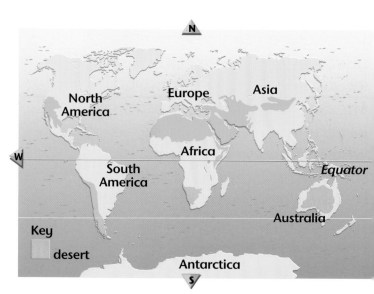

Key

☐ desert

▲ The world's largest desert is in northern Africa. It is called the Sahara.

▲ Some desert land is covered with sand, which the wind blows into hills called dunes. These can be as high as tall office buildings.

◄ Monument Valley in Arizona and Utah is a rocky desert. It is covered with gravel and stones. Columns of bare rock rise toward the sky.

Desert plants

Sometimes, desert plants have to survive several years with almost no rain. They store water inside their leaves, roots, or stems to stay alive. These plants often have leathery or waxy leaves, which help to keep the water from escaping.

Growing deserts

Today, many people live on land at the edges of deserts. They **graze** their animals on the grass that grows here and clear bushes to plant their crops. But the soil here is light, so in dry years the wind blows it away. This turns the land into desert where little can grow.

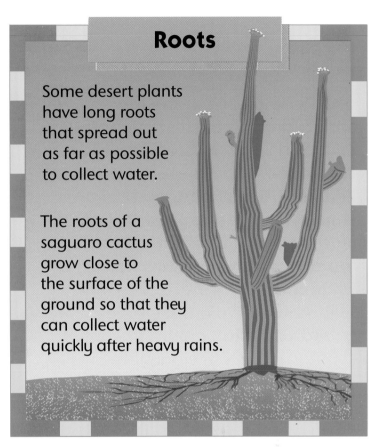

Roots

Some desert plants have long roots that spread out as far as possible to collect water.

The roots of a saguaro cactus grow close to the surface of the ground so that they can collect water quickly after heavy rains.

▼ Nomadic peoples have lived in deserts for thousands of years, moving their animals from place to place to find food and water.

Polar lands

The polar lands lie at the far north and south of Earth, near the North and South **Poles**. They are cold places, with **temperatures** well below freezing for most of the year. The part of Earth around the North Pole is called the Arctic. Most of it is frozen ocean. The part around the South Pole is called Antarctica. It is a windy, icy land with high mountains.

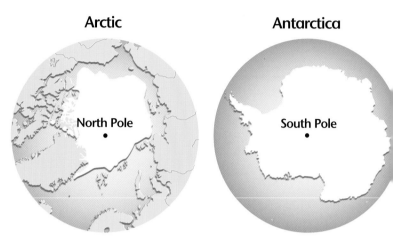

Arctic · Antarctica

North Pole

South Pole

▲ This is how the Arctic and Antarctica would look if you were flying in a rocket above the Poles.

▼ The polar lands are covered with a thick sheet of ice. Icebergs are huge chunks of ice that break off the ice sheet and crash into the ocean.

Life in the freezer

Many kinds of animals live in the polar lands. Foxes and reindeer make their homes on the frozen Arctic plains, called tundra, while around Antarctica whales, seals, and penguins swim in the ocean. Few animals live on the ice at the North and South Poles because the weather here is too cold.

▼ Walruses are large seals. They have a thick layer of fat, called blubber, under their skin to keep them warm.

Did you know?

Every year Arctic terns fly from the Arctic to Antarctica and back again. Terns live for about 20 years, so in their lives, they travel the same distance as to the Moon and back!

The only warm spot in Antarctica is Mount Erebus, an active volcano.

In Antarctica, the ice can be over 2 miles thick. You would have to pile up ten Empire State Buildings to reach the top.

▲ Thousands of tourists visit Antarctica on cruise ships each year.

Learning about Antarctica

No one lives in Antarctica, but scientists visit for months at a time. They stay in research stations, studying the land and its animals. The clear skies above the Poles have helped scientists to make discoveries about the air around Earth.

Earthquake

An earthquake is a shaking of the ground caused by a sudden movement in Earth's crust. An earthquake can be so slight that nobody notices or strong enough to destroy whole buildings. Powerful earthquakes are rare.

Where earthquakes happen

Most earthquakes happen in places where Earth's crust has cracked, making a weak spot called a fault line. Some large fault lines lie above the places where Earth's **plates** meet. Many fault lines lie along the ocean bed, but a few can be seen on land.

▶ The San Andreas Fault in California is one of Earth's biggest fault lines.

Why earthquakes happen

Many powerful earthquakes begin underground at the edges of Earth's plates. Sometimes the plates push against each other. The crust above has to stand a great strain.

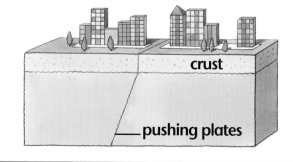

Suddenly the plates shift. This sends out powerful **shock waves**, which travel through the crust and make the ground above shake. Cracks may appear on Earth's surface.

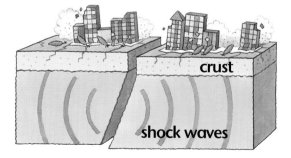

Under the sea

Earthquakes can happen under the sea. The shock waves push the water into giant sea waves, called tsunami, which can travel twice as fast as a race car. The waves grow taller as they reach the shore. They can destroy towns along the coast.

▼ Falling buildings can be dangerous. People who live near fault lines try to strengthen their buildings to keep them from collapsing during earthquakes.

Measuring earthquakes

Scientists study an earthquake by measuring the strength of its shock waves on the Richter **scale**. The scale runs from 1 to 10. Part of the Richter scale is shown below.

3. Barely felt. Some hanging objects may swing.

5. Felt by all. Windows shatter and walls may crack.

6. Serious damage. Cracks open up in the ground.

8. Can cause total damage to buildings. Landscape changes.

Volcano

A volcano is an opening in Earth's crust from which ash, **gas**, and hot rock can **erupt**. Volcanoes that erupt regularly are called active. Some volcanoes are dormant, which means they have not erupted for a long time. Volcanoes that will never erupt again are called **extinct**.

Did you know?

There are about 500 active volcanoes on land, but many more lie under the sea.

There are volcanoes on other **planets**. On Mars, Olympus Mons is a volcano three times the size of Mount Everest.

The rocks near a volcano are warm. Maori people in New Zealand once cooked their food in "ovens" in the hot ground.

How a volcano erupts

Under Earth's crust there is hot **liquid** rock called magma. Sometimes, a mixture of magma and gas pushes its way out of a weak spot in Earth's crust. This is how a volcano erupts.

❷ The magma shoots out. It is now called lava.

❸ The lava cools and hardens. Layers of lava slowly build up.

❶ Magma gathers below the crust.

Looking at lava

When lava pours out of a volcano, it burns everything in its path. Thick lava moves at a walking pace, but thin lava streams down faster than a person can run. It may travel several miles before it cools.

▲ Lava is more than eight times hotter than boiling water. It hardens into wrinkled folds of dark rock.

▼ Scientists watch a volcano erupt from the safety of a helicopter. Eruptions such as these make it difficult for plants and animals to live near an active volcano.

▲ Experts, called vulcanologists, test the rocks and gases near an active volcano to help them predict when it will erupt.

Air

Air is a mixture of invisible **gases** all around us. One of these gases, called **oxygen**, is important because animals and people need it to breathe. Without oxygen, they could not survive. A layer of air surrounds Earth. It is called the atmosphere.

The atmosphere

The atmosphere protects Earth in two important ways. During the day, it blocks out dangerous rays from the burning Sun. At night, it holds in the day's heat like a blanket and helps keep the **planet** warm.

◄ Air fills the skydiver's parachute and helps slow down her fall.

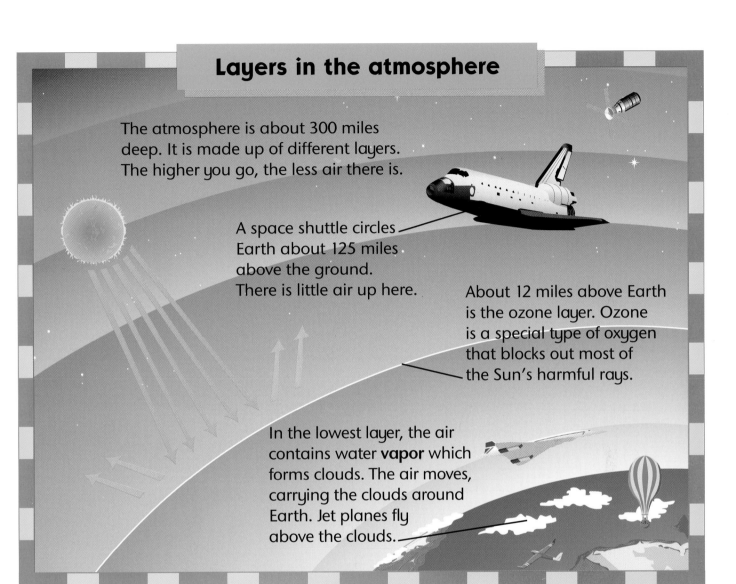

Layers in the atmosphere

The atmosphere is about 300 miles deep. It is made up of different layers. The higher you go, the less air there is.

A space shuttle circles Earth about 125 miles above the ground. There is little air up here.

About 12 miles above Earth is the ozone layer. Ozone is a special type of oxygen that blocks out most of the Sun's harmful rays.

In the lowest layer, the air contains water **vapor** which forms clouds. The air moves, carrying the clouds around Earth. Jet planes fly above the clouds.

Air pollution

Smoke from factories and fumes from cars and trucks damage the air by filling it with harmful gases. This is called air pollution. Polluted air harms many plants and animals. It can cause breathing problems for children and older people.

▶ Air is full of tiny specks, such as **pollen** grains, that people cannot see. These pollen grains have been enlarged under a **microscope**.

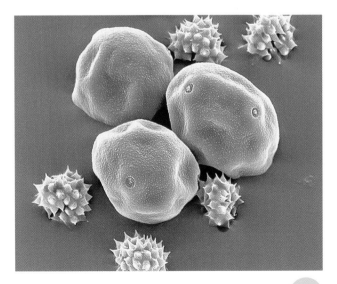

Wind

Wind is moving air. It can be a gentle breeze or as strong as a hurricane. People cannot see the wind, but they can feel it on their cheeks or watch it blow the clouds along. Winds are always blowing around Earth, and they bring changes in the weather. A warm day can suddenly turn cold if winds blow in from a cooler area.

▶ A strong wind can fill a sail with air and drive a windsurfer across the water at high speeds.

Why does the wind blow?

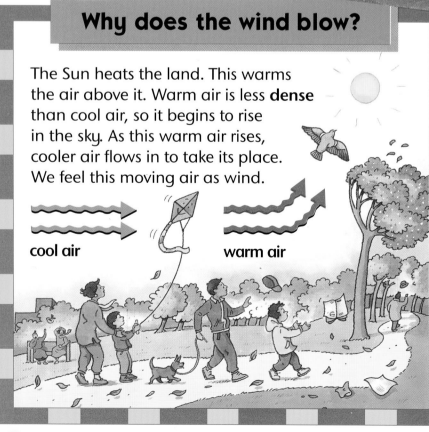

The Sun heats the land. This warms the air above it. Warm air is less **dense** than cool air, so it begins to rise in the sky. As this warm air rises, cooler air flows in to take its place. We feel this moving air as wind.

cool air   warm air

Using the wind

Moving air has **energy**, which people use in many ways. The wind can dry wet laundry on a line. It can also turn the sails of a windmill. In the past, windmills worked machines that ground grain into flour or pumped water on or off the land.

▼ On a wind farm, large numbers of modern windmills work together, using the wind to make **electricity** for nearby towns.

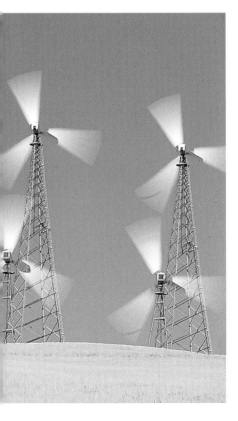

Measuring the wind

Scientists can measure the strength of the wind with the Beaufort **scale**. It runs from force 0 to force 12.

Force 0: Calm. Chimney smoke rises straight up.

Force 5: Fresh wind. Small trees sway. Litter is blown around.

Force 12: Hurricane. This is rare. Houses are destroyed and forests flattened.

Hurricanes

Some winds blow so strongly that they are dangerous. Hurricanes are large storms with strong spinning winds. They start over warm seas but move quickly toward the land. Hurricanes also bring heavy rain, which **floods** the land.

▶ The wind can pick up dust and sand from the ground to make a small spinning storm called a dust devil.

Water

There is water almost everywhere on Earth. It is in rivers, **lakes**, and the ocean, and even under the ground in soil and rocks. It also falls from the sky as rain and snow. Water has no color, taste, or smell, and it comes in different forms. It is often a **liquid**, which people can drink, but it can also be a **gas** or a **solid**.

▲ About two-thirds of your body is made of water. Human beings and most animals need to drink plenty of water every day.

The water cycle

The world's water moves from the land and ocean to the sky and back again. This movement is called the water cycle.

2 Air cools as it rises. It becomes so cold that the water vapor changes back into droplets of water. These form clouds.

1 The Sun's heat changes water from the land and ocean into a gas called water **vapor**. This mixes with the air and rises into the sky.

Ice and snow

When water becomes very cold, it freezes, turning into a solid called ice. As soon as ice is warmed up, it becomes water again.

Snow is a type of ice made high up in the clouds. If the air is cold enough, water droplets in the clouds freeze into crystals of ice. The ice crystals fall as snow.

▲ On cold winter days, dripping water can freeze into long, thin icicles on roofs, doors, and window frames.

❸ The droplets grow bigger until they are too heavy to float. They fall to the ground as rain.

Running out of water

In some parts of the world, there is little rainfall, and in the driest years there may be a **drought**. Many countries try to avoid water shortages by storing water in huge lakes, called reservoirs, or by taking it from wetter places far away using long pipes.

❹ Rainwater trickles into rivers and flows downhill, back into the ocean.

See also Ocean, River, Rock, Water, Wind; ANIMALS AND NATURE Seashore

Erosion

Erosion is the removal of land that has been worn away by wind, running water, or ice. On Earth, nothing stays the same. Every rock, hill, mountain, and cliff slowly changes as grains of rock are swept away.

▶ In dry places, the wind picks up fine sand and hurls it at the rocks, slowly carving them into wonderful shapes.

Raging rivers

Rivers change the shape of the land by wearing away the rock as the water flows over it. As a fast-flowing river moves along, it picks up stones and pebbles, which chip away at the banks and riverbed. Eventually this pounding and chipping cuts **valleys** and **gorges** into the hillside.

◀ The Grand Canyon took millions of years to form. The Colorado River cut a deep gorge in the land.

Grinding glaciers

Glaciers are rivers of ice. They form on high land when layers of snow become packed into hard ice. Eventually glaciers become so heavy they begin to slide slowly downhill.

▶ A glacier scrapes away at the ground beneath, leaving behind a smooth, U-shaped valley.

Pounding waves

Ocean cliffs are battered by pounding waves. Over thousands of years, cliffs crumble and crack, forming caves and different-shaped rocks. The movement of the waves also sweeps sand or pebbles along the shore and changes the shape of the beach.

Fighting erosion

Strong winds or heavy rains can carry away soil that is good for farming. In some places, people plant trees to keep this from happening. The tree roots hold the soil together. On hillsides, people cut big steps into the farmland to keep the soil from washing downhill.

▶ An arch has formed where the ocean has eroded an area of rock.

Day and night

Nearly all of the light on Earth comes from the Sun. But the Sun can shine only on one half of Earth at a time. This part of Earth has daytime. The part of Earth that faces away from the Sun has nighttime. This is why time on Earth follows a pattern of days and nights.

Light and dark

Earth is a **planet** spinning in space. It turns like a top, taking 24 hours to go around once. Most places on Earth have daylight for about half of these hours. The other hours are in darkness.

nighttime

daytime

Sun

Earth

The Sun is always shining in space, even if people cannot see it.

Keeping time

Before clocks were invented, people guessed the time of day by looking at the position of the Sun in the sky. Today, we have clocks that tell the time exactly, down to the last second.

▼ One way to tell the time is to measure the shadow made by the Sun on a sundial.

▲ Modern clocks need to be accurate. Less than a second can make the difference between winning and losing a race.

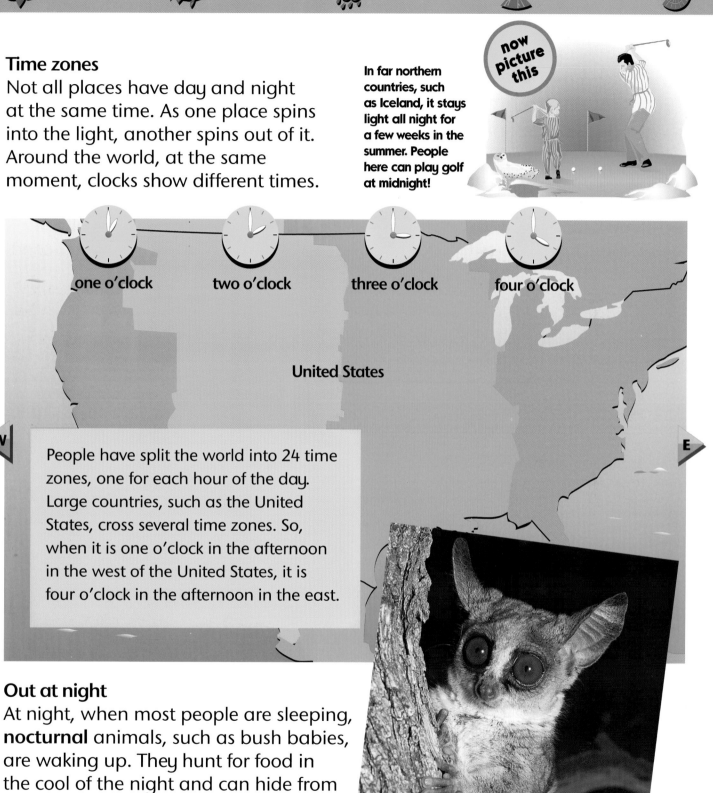

Time zones

Not all places have day and night at the same time. As one place spins into the light, another spins out of it. Around the world, at the same moment, clocks show different times.

In far northern countries, such as Iceland, it stays light all night for a few weeks in the summer. People here can play golf at midnight!

now picture this

one o'clock   two o'clock   three o'clock   four o'clock

United States

W

E

People have split the world into 24 time zones, one for each hour of the day. Large countries, such as the United States, cross several time zones. So, when it is one o'clock in the afternoon in the west of the United States, it is four o'clock in the afternoon in the east.

Out at night

At night, when most people are sleeping, **nocturnal** animals, such as bush babies, are waking up. They hunt for food in the cool of the night and can hide from their enemies more easily in the dark.

▶ Many nocturnal animals have large eyes, which help them see well in the dark.

51

See also Polar lands; A FIRST ATLAS Southern Asia; ANIMALS AND NATURE Season, Weather

Climate and season

Climate is a pattern of weather that is roughly the same every year. Everywhere on Earth has its own climate. The climate of a particular place depends mainly on where it is in the world.

Around the world

Places near the **Equator** have a **tropical** climate. They are hot all year round. Near the **Poles**, the climate is always cold. In between, there are places that have a temperate climate. This means the weather here is rarely very hot or very cold.

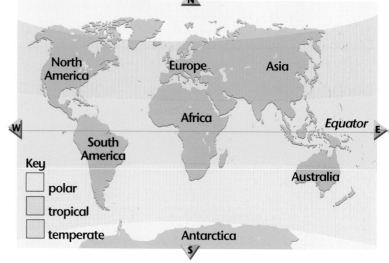

Key
- polar
- tropical
- temperate

▲ This map shows where polar, temperate, and tropical climates are found in the world.

now picture this

If Earth's climate suddenly became warmer, the ice near the Poles would melt. The ocean would rise, and cities, such as New York, would be underwater.

▶ Wherever people live, they have to **adapt** to the climate. In cold parts of the world, people wear warm clothes to keep out the bitter winds.

Four seasons

In most places, the weather changes throughout the year. These changes are called seasons. In temperate areas, there are four seasons. Winter is cold with many frosty nights. In spring, days become brighter. In summer, there are warm days with lots of sunshine. Cooler weather returns in autumn.

Wet and dry

Some tropical areas have only two seasons in the year, one wet and one dry. In the wet season, strong winds bring clouds and rain. This is called a monsoon. In the dry season, the weather is hot and the ground is dry.

▲ During cold winter months, animals, such as dormice, fall into a deep sleep called hibernation. They wake up again when spring arrives.

▲ During a monsoon, heavy rain can cause problems because it **floods** city streets.

Microscopic life

All living things are made up of tiny building blocks called cells. Human beings are made of **billions** of cells, but many microscopic creatures are made of only one. They are so small that they are invisible to human eyes. People can see them only if they look through a **microscope**.

Bacteria

Bacteria are tiny living things. They are found in the air, on the ground, and on animals and plants. Some bacteria are harmful. They spoil food or cause tooth decay. Others are helpful and are used to make medicines, soaps, and cheeses.

▲ A microscope can make things look many times larger than they really are.

Algae

Algae are simple living things that are found in **lakes**, ponds, and the ocean. Many use sunlight to make their food and to grow. Some algae can be seen only under a microscope and have only one cell. Other types of algae, such as seaweed, grow large and have many cells.

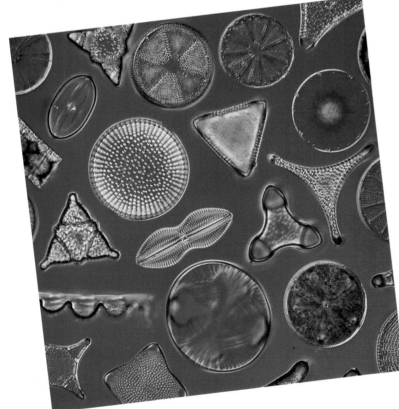

◄ Microscopic algae are an important food for other water creatures.

Feeding on others

Many microscopic creatures live on or inside plants and animals and feed on them. They are called parasites. Some parasites even live inside humans. Most parasites are harmless, but a few, such as some types of bacteria, can cause diseases.

Did you know?

People have thousands of bacteria living inside their stomachs. The bacteria feed by helping to break down the food people eat into smaller pieces.

Scientists could study tiny living things only after the microscope was invented in the 1600s.

Tiny mites live on some people's eyelashes.

▲ Dust mites live in carpets and feed on specks of dead skin that fall off people's bodies. This dust mite is shown nearly 500 times larger than it really is.

Plant

Plants are living things that grow on Earth. They come in many shapes and sizes, from tiny flowers to huge trees. Unlike animals, plants do not move about to find food. They make their own food using air, sunlight, and water.

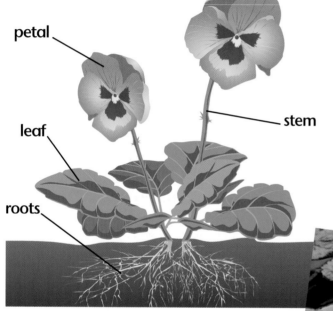

petal

stem

leaf

roots

▲ Plants may look different from each other, but most have similar parts.

All kinds of plants

There are nearly 400,000 different kinds of plants. Some, such as grasses, grow on almost every type of land. Scientists divide plants into groups. Two large groups are flowering plants, such as apple trees and daisies, and non-flowering plants, such as mosses and ferns.

▲ The stem of a tree is called a trunk. As a tree gets older, its trunk grows thicker.

◄ Water plants, such as lilies, have tiny air holes in their stems. These keep them upright in the water.

Making food

A plant takes in a **gas** called carbon dioxide from the air. It uses the carbon dioxide, **energy** from the Sun, and water from the ground to make food, which helps it to grow.

Making seeds

A flower is the part of a plant that makes seeds. To grow seeds, a flower has to spread a dust, called **pollen**, to another flower. This is called pollination. Some insects pick up grains of pollen which they carry to other flowers. Later, the seeds grow into new plants.

▲ A bee's body is covered in tiny hairs which collect pollen as the bee crawls over a flower.

Seeds on the move

After pollination, a plant's seeds begin to grow. Plants spread their seeds in many ways.

Many seeds grow in a juicy fruit. Animals eat the fruit, and the seeds pass out in their droppings.

Some seeds grow in a pod. As the pod dries out, it splits open, flicking its seeds far and wide.

Coconuts are huge seeds that drop from palm trees and float across the sea to other beaches.

Dandelion seeds float through the air on a tuft of fine hair.

Plants as food

For thousands of years, people have been growing plants for their food. People eat many different parts of plants. For example, carrots and potatoes are roots. Asparagus and celery are stems. Lettuces are leaves. Cauliflower and broccoli are flowers. Apples and bananas are fruits, and rice is a seed.

Insect

An insect is a small animal with six legs. It has no backbone and belongs to a group of creatures called **invertebrates**. An insect has a hard case, called an exoskeleton, on the outside of its body. It sheds its exoskeleton as it grows. Insects have wings and most can fly.

All sorts of insects

There are over one million different kinds of insects, and new ones are discovered every year. Insects live all over the world and in every kind of place except the ocean. Fleas, flies, butterflies, and bees are all insects.

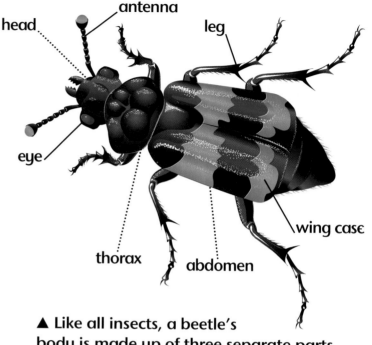

head antenna leg

eye

thorax abdomen wing case

▲ Like all insects, a beetle's body is made up of three separate parts. They are a head, a thorax, and an abdomen.

▼ Many insects, such as damselflies, have two pairs of wings instead of one.

A good defense

Insects must protect themselves from the many animals that feed on them. Some insects use **camouflage**, which helps them to hide from their enemies. Others frighten their attackers with scary markings or painful stings.

▶ A flower mantis hides itself by looking like part of the plant where it rests.

Growing up

The shape of an insect changes completely as it grows. This way of growing is called metamorphosis.

❶ A female ant lays lots of tiny white eggs.

❷ After a few days, the eggs hatch into worm-like larvae, which feed and grow.

❸ The larvae become pupae by growing hard cases around themselves. Inside, the pupa changes.

❹ A few weeks later, an adult ant crawls out.

Did you know?

The Goliath beetle of Central Africa weighs three times more than a mouse. It is the heaviest insect in the world.

A queen honey bee can lay 2,000 eggs a day for her whole life.

Insects have blood in their bodies, but it's not red like the blood of most animals. Instead, it is greenish yellow.

Friend or foe?

Insects help plants make seeds and are an important food for other animals. They also clean the land by feeding on dead animals and plants. But some insects can be real pests. They spread disease, destroy crops, and damage houses, furniture, and clothes.

Fish

A fish is a type of creature that lives in water. It has a backbone and belongs to a group of animals called **vertebrates**. Most fish have fins and a tail for swimming, and body parts, called gills, for breathing underwater. Fish feed on many different animals and plants. Some kinds of fish live in the ocean, but others live in freshwater **lakes** and streams.

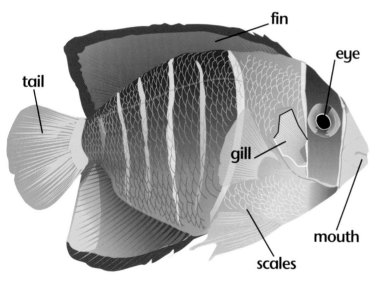

tail

fin

eye

gill

mouth

scales

▲ Most fish have scales that overlap each other and protect the fish's body.

How a fish breathes

The world's ocean, lakes, and rivers all contain **oxygen**, which a fish needs to breathe in order to survive. As a fish swims along, it gulps in mouthfuls of water, which flow through its gills. Inside the gills, the oxygen in the water passes into the fish's blood.

How a fish moves

A fish ripples through the water by squeezing the muscles on the sides of its body, one side at a time. Most fish also beat their tails from side to side to give themselves an extra push. They use their fins to steer through the water and keep their balance.

▼ Many fish, such as these sea bream, live in large groups called schools.

From egg to fish

Most fish hatch out of eggs. Some fish lay thousands of eggs at a time. They may lay their eggs in gravel on a riverbed or let them float in the water. Many of the eggs are eaten by other animals, but some survive and hatch into tiny fish.

▼ Three or four months after the eggs are laid, the baby salmon hatch.

Did you know?

South American piranhas are the most ferocious fish in the world. They will attack any creature, no matter how big, especially if it is injured or splashing in the water.

Flying fish can take off and glide up to 300 feet through the air.

The dwarf goby is the smallest fish in the ocean. It's about the size of a fingernail.

Good protection

Fish have many enemies, including larger fish, seals, and birds. One way they try to protect themselves is by hiding. Some fish dig holes on the ocean floor, while others lie **camouflaged** against the bottom.

▼ A puffer fish scares its enemies by puffing itself up and sticking out its spines.

Amphibian

An amphibian is an animal that lives on land but lays its eggs in a pond or river. Its young live here for several weeks until they are old enough to leave the water. Amphibians live in all the continents of the world except for Antarctica.

Frogs and toads

Frogs and toads are the largest group of amphibians. Frogs live near ponds and streams. They have smooth, moist skin and long back legs. Their nostrils are high on their heads so they can breathe as they swim. Toads are similar to frogs, but they have shorter back legs and dry bumpy skin.

webbed foot

leg

▲ A frog has strong legs for jumping and webbed feet for swimming.

nostril

eye

Newts and salamanders

Newts and salamanders are a small group of amphibians. Unlike frogs and toads, they have thin bodies and long tails. They catch worms and insects by flicking out their long sticky tongues.

▼ Salamanders live in cool damp places, such as rotting tree stumps or at the bottom of streams and rivers.

▲ Toads live most of their lives on land and only return to the water to lay their eggs.

Colorful signals

Amphibians are eaten by many kinds of animals, including birds and fish. To protect themselves, some have foul-tasting poisons in their skin. They are also often brightly colored, which warns other animals not to come too close.

▶ **A bright green tree frog uses its sticky toes to cling to branches.**

Life cycle of a toad

The shape of an amphibian changes completely as it grows.
This way of growing is called metamorphosis.

❶ A female toad lays long strings of eggs in a pond or river. The strings are called toad spawn.

❷ The eggs hatch into tadpoles, which breathe **oxygen** in the water through gills under their skin.

❸ After a few weeks, each tadpole begins to grow legs. Later, its tail shrinks and disappears.

❹ When a toad is fully grown, it leaves the water to live on land. It can now breathe air.

Reptile

A reptile is an animal that has a dry scaly body. Its young usually hatch from eggs. There are about 6,500 different kinds of reptiles. Most live in warm parts of the world.

Hot and cold

A reptile is a cold-blooded animal. This means the **temperature** of its body is the same as the air around it. To stay alive, a reptile must not get too hot or too cold. To warm up, it lies in the sun. To cool down, a reptile finds a shady spot or goes for a swim.

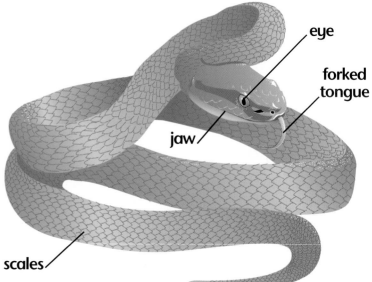

eye

forked tongue

jaw

scales

▲ A snake has no legs, but it can still move quickly. Many snakes can burrow, climb trees, swim, and a few can even glide through the air.

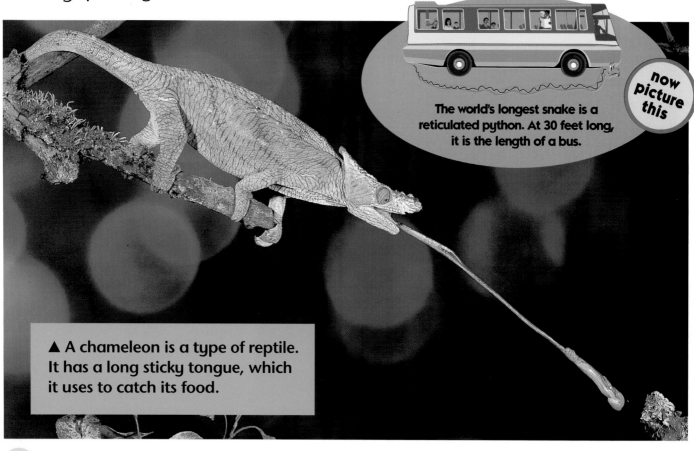

The world's longest snake is a reticulated python. At 30 feet long, it is the length of a bus.

now picture this

▲ A chameleon is a type of reptile. It has a long sticky tongue, which it uses to catch its food.

Reptile families

The largest group of reptiles is made up of lizards and snakes. Most of these feed on other animals. Another group of reptiles is tortoises and turtles. They both have shells, but tortoises live on land and turtles live in water. Crocodiles and alligators are also reptiles that live in water.

Did you know?

Dinosaurs were reptiles. They also laid eggs and had scaly skin. But most of them had longer legs and could run faster than reptiles today.

Giant tortoises can live to be more than 100 years old.

Many lizards can lose their tails. If an animal grabs a lizard by the tail, the end breaks off and the lizard can run to safety. A new tail soon grows back.

◄ Crocodiles are fierce creatures, with strong jaws full of sharp teeth. They eat mainly fish and smaller reptiles.

Baby reptiles

Most reptiles, even those that live in water, lay their eggs in a nest on land.

1 A female turtle swims ashore to lay her eggs in the sand.

2 She uses her back feet to cover the eggs with sand. Then, she returns to the sea.

3 Weeks later, tiny turtles hatch out of the eggs, looking much like their parents.

4 The turtles race into the sea, where they live and grow.

Bird

A bird is an animal with feathers, wings, and a beak. Its young hatch from eggs. There are more than 9,000 different kinds of birds, and they come in many shapes and sizes. They live in all parts of the world, from the **tropics** to the **Poles.** Birds are found in forests, on mountain tops, by rivers and seas, in deserts, and in cities.

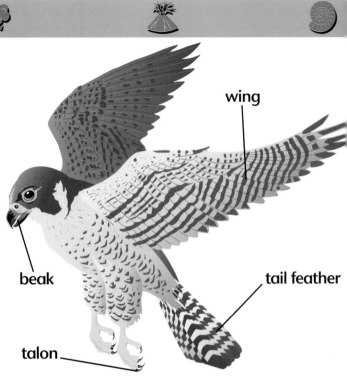

wing

beak

talon

tail feather

▲ Some birds have sharp claws, called talons, which they use to catch other animals.

▶ A puffin lives by the ocean. It has webbed feet that help it to swim. It uses its large beak to scoop fish out of the water.

On the wing

A bird's strong wings help it find food and escape from danger. Some birds, such as snow geese, fly long distances every year to avoid the cold winter months. This is called migration. A few birds cannot fly. An ostrich is too heavy to leave the ground, but it has long legs that help it run fast instead.

now picture this

An ostrich is the largest living bird. At 8 feet tall, it can look down on the tallest human.

Fine feathers

A bird takes great care of its feathers which help it fly and keep it warm and dry. The top layer of a bird's feathers is oily and waterproof. The bottom layer is fluffy and warm.

▶ **Many male birds have colorful feathers that help them attract female birds.**

Nests and eggs

Birds lay their eggs in nests or other safe places. Most birds sit on their eggs to keep them warm. Inside the eggs, the baby birds, called chicks, feed on the egg yolk and begin to grow. The chicks hatch by pecking their way through the shells.

▼ Most birds are born blind and with only a few feathers. Their parents care for them until they are able to leave the nest.

Did you know?

Large birds, such as swans, can have up to 25,000 feathers.

The Cuban bee hummingbird is the smallest bird in the world. It is just over 2 inches long and its nest is the size of a walnut shell.

Penguins are birds. They cannot fly, but they use their wings to help them swim through the water at great speeds.

Mammal

A mammal is an animal that is hairy and feeds on its mother's milk. It is warm-blooded, which means the **temperature** of its body is nearly always the same. There are about 4,500 different kinds of mammals in the world. Most of them live on land, but some, such as whales and dolphins, live in the ocean. Humans are also mammals.

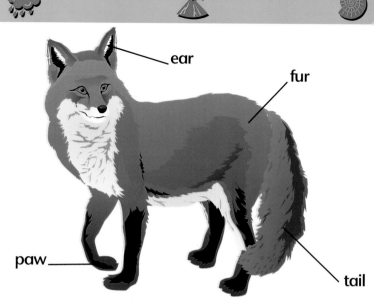

ear

fur

paw

tail

▲ Most mammals have a good sense of hearing. A fox can hear a mouse squeak more than 100 feet away.

◄ Unlike fish, mammals cannot breathe underwater. A whale has to swim up to the surface to take in air.

Eating habits

The type of teeth a mammal has are a clue to the kind of food it eats. Horses and cows are plant-eaters. They have large flat teeth to grind down grasses.

Tigers are meat-eaters. They have long pointed teeth to grip and tear their food. An anteater has no teeth at all. It eats insects, such as ants, which it picks up using its long sticky tongue.

Growing up

A baby mammal grows inside its mother's body. When it is born, it is usually blind and helpless. It grows quickly by drinking its mother's milk, but it may be months, or years, before it can look after itself.

▲ Young lions play-fight with their parents to learn the skills they will need to survive alone in the wild.

▼ A baby kangaroo leaves its mother's pouch when it is about six months old. But it may return at the first sign of danger.

Unusual mammals

Mammals that have a pouch for their young to grow in are called marsupials. A kangaroo is tiny when it is born, only the size of a peanut. Immediately after birth, the baby kangaroo, called a joey, crawls into its mother's pouch. It stays there for many weeks, feeding on her milk.

See also Mammal, Tropical rainforest, Wind; ALL ABOUT PEOPLE

Human

A human belongs to a group of animals called mammals. There are now nearly six **billion** humans, and they live almost everywhere on Earth. They all need air, food, water, and space to live. Humans are also intelligent. They can look after Earth's **natural resources** and the other things that live on Earth.

Around the world

Humans in one part of the world look and live a little differently from those in others. This is because humans have been divided by mountains, deserts, and oceans. Modern transportation, such as airplanes, means that more and more humans are traveling around Earth and sharing their different ways of life.

A different kind of animal

Humans are different from other animals. They have well-developed brains, which they use to solve difficult problems and to invent new things. Humans enjoy reading and talking. They like to discuss questions and ideas.

▶ Many humans enjoy painting pictures of the world around them.

▼ Tokyo, the capital of Japan, is one of the most crowded cities in the world. Many people here live in small apartments.

Changing the world

Over thousands of years, humans have changed the world. They have cut down forests and cleared land to grow food and build cities. Humans have used much of Earth's coal and oil to make **energy** to drive their machines. These changes have often been harmful to plants and animals.

now picture this

Some humans are harming the rainforests. In the time it takes to read this fact, an area the size of ten soccer fields will have been cut down.

A brighter future

Humans are trying to protect Earth. They are finding new kinds of energy and caring for the plants and animals that remain. They want Earth to be a better place where people and animals can live.

▲ Humans are repairing some of the damage done to Earth by planting new trees.

Glossary

Adapt When a living thing changes gradually in order to survive. Nearly all living things have adapted to changes in the world around them.

Bacteria A group of microscopic living things. Some kinds of bacteria can cause disease while others help people.

Billion A number meaning one thousand million, written as 1,000,000,000.

Camouflage The colors and markings on a living thing that help it blend in with its surroundings. An animal can hide easily from other animals if it is well camouflaged.

Coral reef A growth of coral that lies below the surface in shallow parts of the ocean. Coral is built by tiny animals called polyps.

Craft A vehicle for traveling in or on water, on land, or in space.

Dense Packed closely together. For example, warm air is less dense than cold air. When cold air becomes warmer, the tiny particles spread out over a larger area.

Drought When it does not rain for a long time and there is not enough water for people and animals to drink or for farmers to water crops.

Electricity A useful form of **energy** that can be changed into heat, light, sound, and mechanical energy.

Energy The ability of living things and machines to move or work.

Environment The surroundings of any living thing.

Equator An imaginary line that circles Earth around its middle.

Erupts Forces out. When a volcano erupts, **gas**, ash, and lava shoot out of it.

Extinct No longer living on Earth. An animal or plant becomes extinct when no more of its kind are left. Volcanoes can also be extinct. An extinct volcano will never **erupt** again.

Fertile Land that is able to produce plenty of good crops.

Floods When an area that is usually dry becomes covered with water.

Forecasts Predictions that tell people what the weather will be like in the hours and days ahead.

Fungi Simple living things, such as mushrooms and molds.

Gas A substance, such as air, that has no shape.

Gorges Narrow **valleys** with high, steep sides. A gorge is formed when layers of rock are slowly worn away by a stream or river.

Graze To feed on grass. Many farmers take their animals to open fields to graze on grass.

Invertebrates Animals that have no backbones.

Lake A large area of water surrounded by land.

Liquid A substance that has no shape of its own, such as running water.

Mainland The main part of a country or continent, and not the islands surrounding it.

Material The substance that an object is made from.

Microscope An instrument that makes small objects appear larger.

Minerals Natural substances, including iron and salt, that are formed in the ground.

Nocturnal Active at night. Nocturnal animals sleep during the day and wake up at night.

Oxygen A **gas** that animals need to breathe in order to survive. Oxygen is one of the gases found in air.

Planets Huge, usually ball-shaped space objects. Earth is one of nine planets that travel around our Sun.

Plates The huge pieces of rock that make up Earth's crust.

Poles The farthest points of north and south on Earth.

Pollen A fine dust made by flowers. When pollen from one flower is carried to another flower, it can cause the plant to make seeds.

Pressure The force of something, for example air or water, pushing against something else.

Resources Useful or valuable things. Natural resources include coal and oil, land, air, and water.

Scale A set of numbers or measurements that people use to measure objects or events.

Shock waves Vibrations that travel through a **material**. For example, shock waves in the ground can be caused by earthquakes.

Solid A **material** that has a set shape and size, even when it is not in a container.

Temperature A measure of how hot or cold something is.

Tropical Found in the hottest parts of the world, near the **Equator**. The tropics are hot areas found on either side of the Equator.

Vapor Droplets of **liquid** floating in the air.

Valleys Low land lying between mountains and hills, which has been slowly worn away by a river, stream, or glacier.

Vertebrates Animals that have backbones.

Index